P9-BIR-731

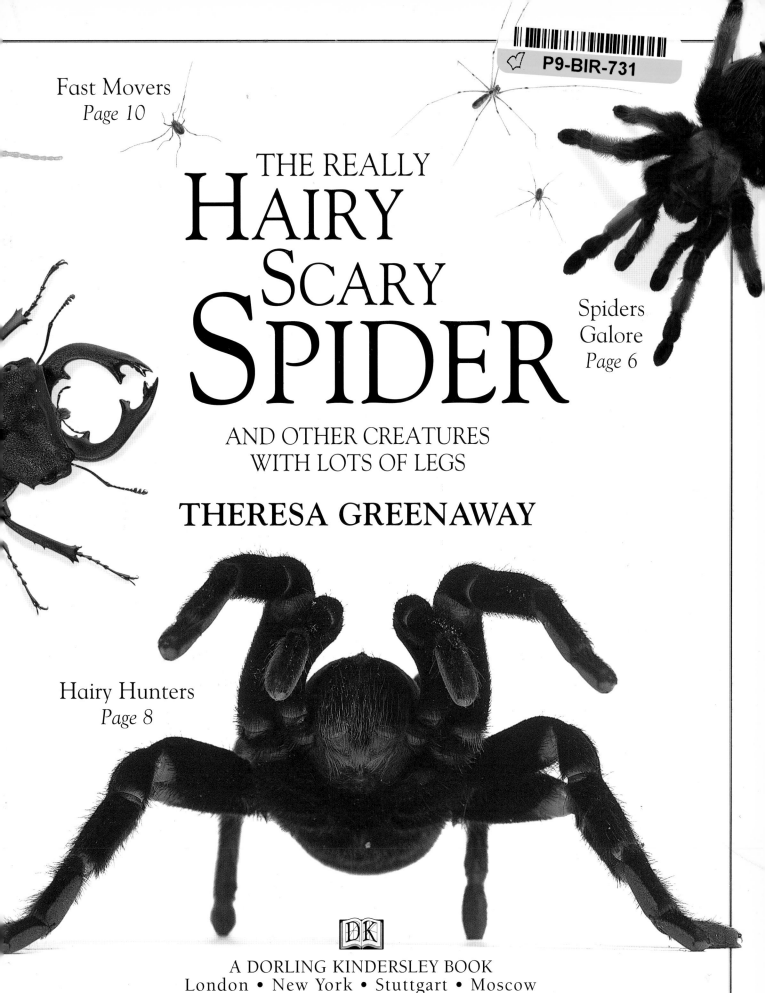

THE REALLY
HAIRY
SCARY
SPIDER

AND OTHER CREATURES
WITH LOTS OF LEGS

THERESA GREENAWAY

A DORLING KINDERSLEY BOOK
London • New York • Stuttgart • Moscow

Jumping spider

SPIDERS GALORE

What is it about spiders that makes us shiver? Is it their hairy bodies, their long legs, or their sticky webs? While these are the features that make them successful hunters, most spiders are unable to give us so much as a harmless nip.

Leaf-mimicking spider

This spider disguises itself as a piece of dead leaf so that prey won't notice it.

Huntsman spider

The deadly funnel-web spider will attack anything that accidentally get in its way. moves, even people,

House spiders actually help us by ridding our homes of insect pests.

House spider

Funnel-web spider

Harvestman

To protect themselves, many spiders paralyse struggling victims with a poisoned bite before tying them up with strong, silk threads.

Daddy-long-legs spider

Tarantula
are sometimes so big their legs can span a dinner plate.

Tarantula

Tarantula

Large spiders, such as this tarantula, can eat frogs, lizards, and even snakes.

HAIRY HUNTERS

Some of the biggest, hairiest spiders of all are actually quite timid. A tarantula would only ever sink its huge fangs into a person in self-defence.

Even though tarantulas have huge bodies, they have very small venom glands.

Tarantula

Tarantula

In spite of having up to eight eyes, most hairy spiders have poor eyesight.

When threatened, tarantulas flick hairs that itch and sting into their enemies faces.

Tarantula

Once a year, a tarantula sheds its skin. When this happens, any hairs lost over the last year are replaced.

Huntsman spiders

Tarantula

Huntsman spiders eat insects such as cockroaches.

Some female tarantulas have been known to live for up to 30 years.

A trapdoor spider lives in a silk-lined tunnel. It peeks out of the slightly open trapdoor lid, waiting to seize any passing insects.

An untreated funnel-web bite is deadly. Fortunately, an antivenin now saves most victims.

Funnel-web spider

A funnel-web's knife-sharp fangs can easily pierce fingernail or bone.

Trapdoor spider

Tarantulas' fangs aren't very venomous. Instead, these spiders crush up prey and then cover them in digestive juices.

Sensitive hairs on its legs warn this spider of approaching danger – or dinner.

Tarantula

A tarantula is a slow eater. It will usually drag its prey back to its burrow before eating it.

FAST MOVERS

We're often startled when a spindly spider suddenly appears, darting up a wall or scuttling across a floor. But, while it may be running very fast, it's probably running away from us.

Harvestman

Daddy-long-legs jump up and down in a frenzy to scare off their enemies.

Daddy-long-legs spider

Daddy-long-legs make messy webs on our ceilings, but they also eat lots of flies.

Orb-web spiders can make enough silk to climb the Eiffel Tower twice.

Orb-web spider

Orb-web spiders recycle old webs by eating them and then spinning new ones.

This spider avoids being eaten by birds by disguising itself as a bad-tasting ant.

Ant-mimicking spider

Orb-web spider

Experts can identify a species of orb-web spider just by looking at the shape of its web.

A house spider could give you a fright by rushing out from under your chair. But it's not after your toes, it's just looking for a mate.

Spider silk is one of the strongest and lightest of all known fibres.

A harvestman isn't a spider. Unlike true spiders, it doesn't have a separate head and body.

Harvestman

House spider

House spiders don't climb up drain pipes, as many people think. If you find one in your bath, it probably just slipped in and couldn't get back out.

Jumping spiders can leap 40 times their body length. That's like a child jumping an Olympic swimming pool.

Jumping spider

COUNT THOSE LEGS

What makes centipedes different from millipedes? Centipedes are carnivores with two legs on each segment; millipedes eat plants and have four legs on each segment.

Some tropical millipedes ooze such smelly poisons over their skin that even the hungriest predators think twice.

Armoured millipede

By eating rotting wood, this armoured millipede helps recycle the nutrients in fallen trees.

Woodland centipede

The woodland centipede's long legs make it a very fast runner.

Garden centipede

Centipedes use their last pair of legs to feel their way when backing out of tight places.

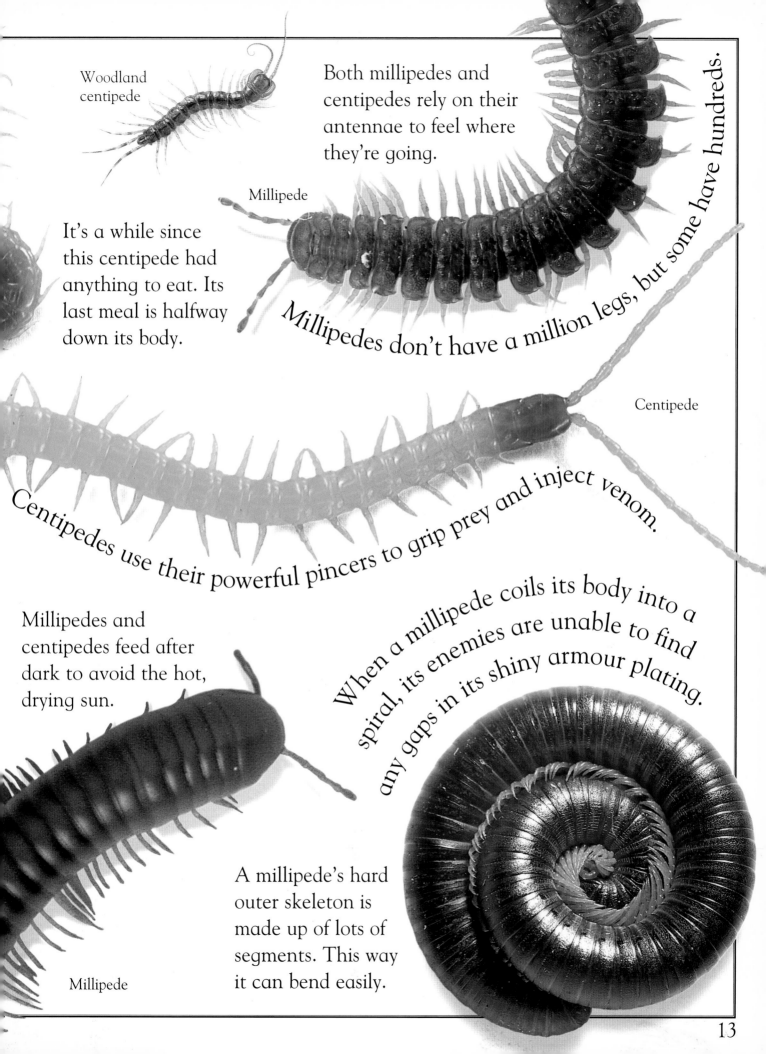

Woodland centipede

Both millipedes and centipedes rely on their antennae to feel where they're going.

Millipede

It's a while since this centipede had anything to eat. Its last meal is halfway down its body.

Millipedes don't have a million legs, but some have hundreds.

Centipede

Centipedes use their powerful pincers to grip prey and inject venom.

Millipedes and centipedes feed after dark to avoid the hot, drying sun.

When a millipede coils its body into a spiral, its enemies are unable to find any gaps in its shiny armour plating.

A millipede's hard outer skeleton is made up of lots of segments. This way it can bend easily.

Millipede

13

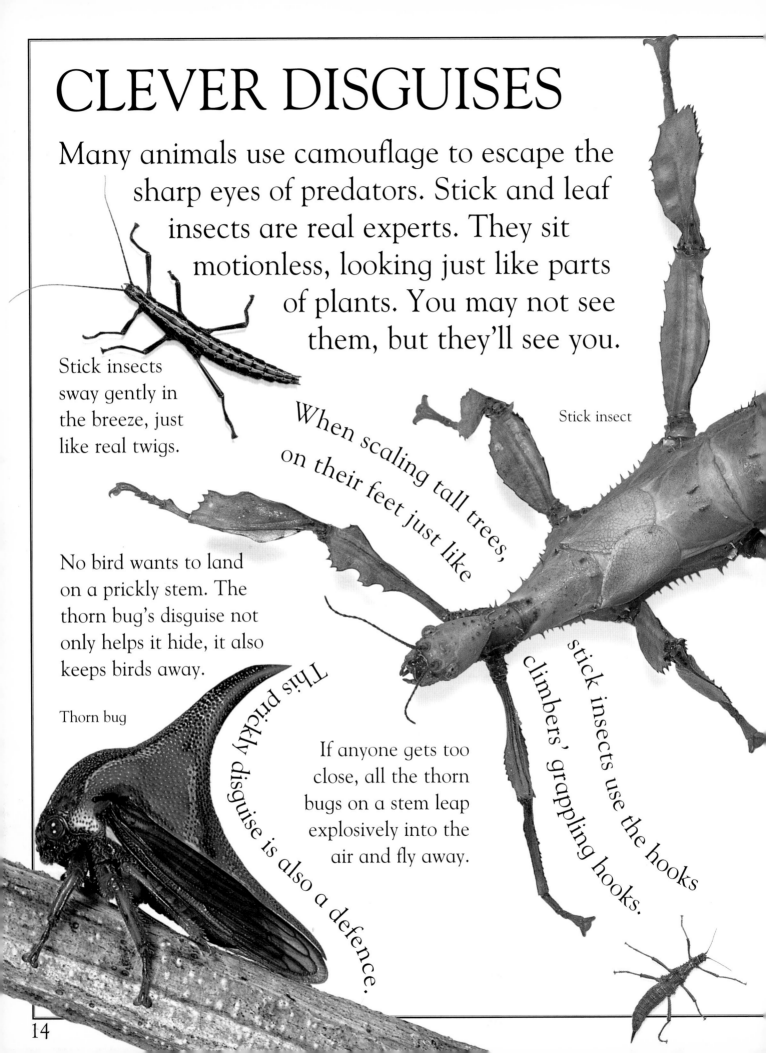

CLEVER DISGUISES

Many animals use camouflage to escape the sharp eyes of predators. Stick and leaf insects are real experts. They sit motionless, looking just like parts of plants. You may not see them, but they'll see you.

Stick insects sway gently in the breeze, just like real twigs.

Stick insect

When scaling tall trees, on their feet just like

No bird wants to land on a prickly stem. The thorn bug's disguise not only helps it hide, it also keeps birds away.

Thorn bug

This prickly disguise is also a defence.

If anyone gets too close, all the thorn bugs on a stem leap explosively into the air and fly away.

stick insects use the hooks climbers' grappling hooks.

14

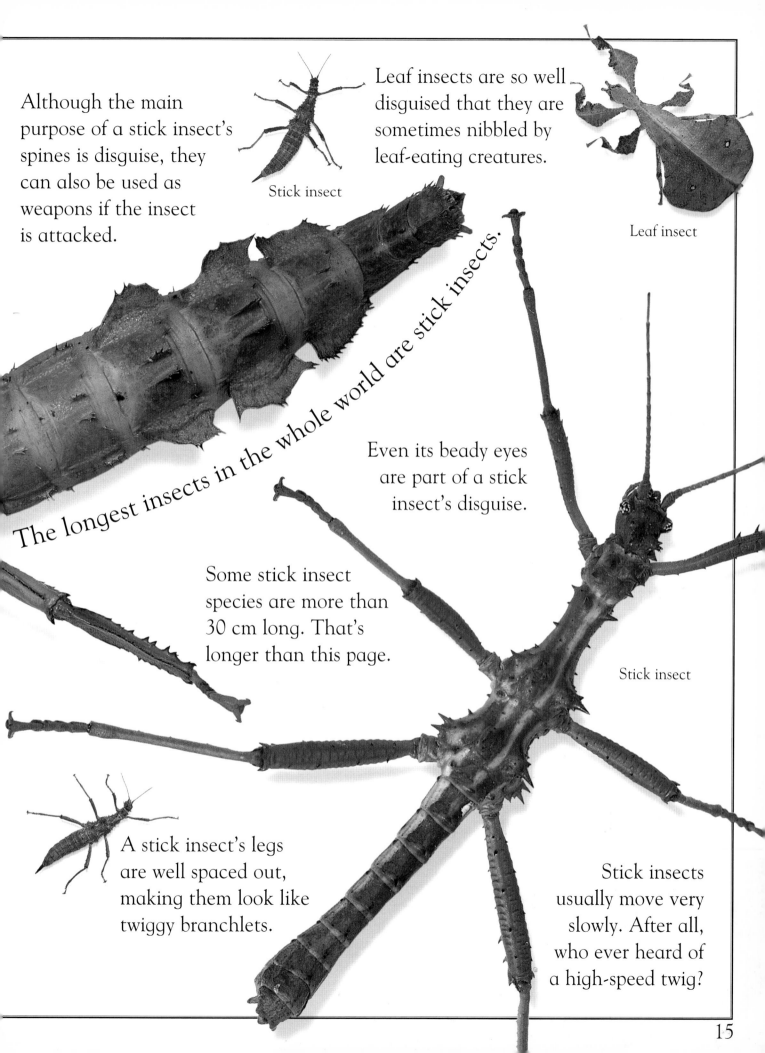

Although the main purpose of a stick insect's spines is disguise, they can also be used as weapons if the insect is attacked.

Stick insect

Leaf insects are so well disguised that they are sometimes nibbled by leaf-eating creatures.

Leaf insect

The longest insects in the whole world are stick insects.

Even its beady eyes are part of a stick insect's disguise.

Some stick insect species are more than 30 cm long. That's longer than this page.

Stick insect

A stick insect's legs are well spaced out, making them look like twiggy branchlets.

Stick insects usually move very slowly. After all, who ever heard of a high-speed twig?

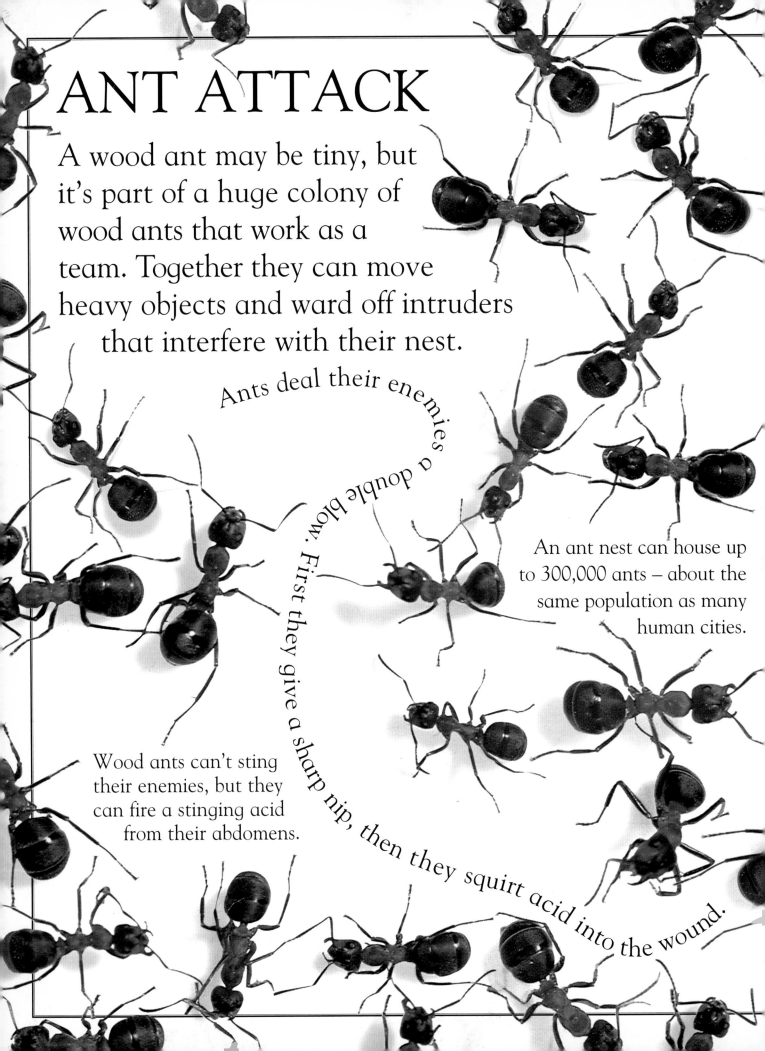

ANT ATTACK

A wood ant may be tiny, but it's part of a huge colony of wood ants that work as a team. Together they can move heavy objects and ward off intruders that interfere with their nest.

Ants deal their enemies a double blow. First they give a sharp nip, then they squirt acid into the wound.

An ant nest can house up to 300,000 ants – about the same population as many human cities.

Wood ants can't sting their enemies, but they can fire a stinging acid from their abdomens.

When an ant finds a dead insect that's too big to carry, lots of others help to break it up and drag it back to the nest.

The food-gathering ants in a nest are called worker ants.

Wood ants help forests by eating leaf-eating insect larvae.

TINY TANKS

There are more than 350,000 kinds of beetles, that's more than any other animal on Earth. Each species is different, but they all have tough wing cases and strong, biting jaws.

Rhinoceros beetle

Rove beetle

This rove beetle cuts up prey with its scissor-like jaws.

Rhinoceros beetles are the world's strongest animals, lifting 850 times their own weight. That's like you carrying 850 of your friends.

Well-armoured male beetles do battle to impress females.

Minotaur beetle

Male minotaur beetles give presents of rabbit droppings to females. The females lay their eggs in the droppings.

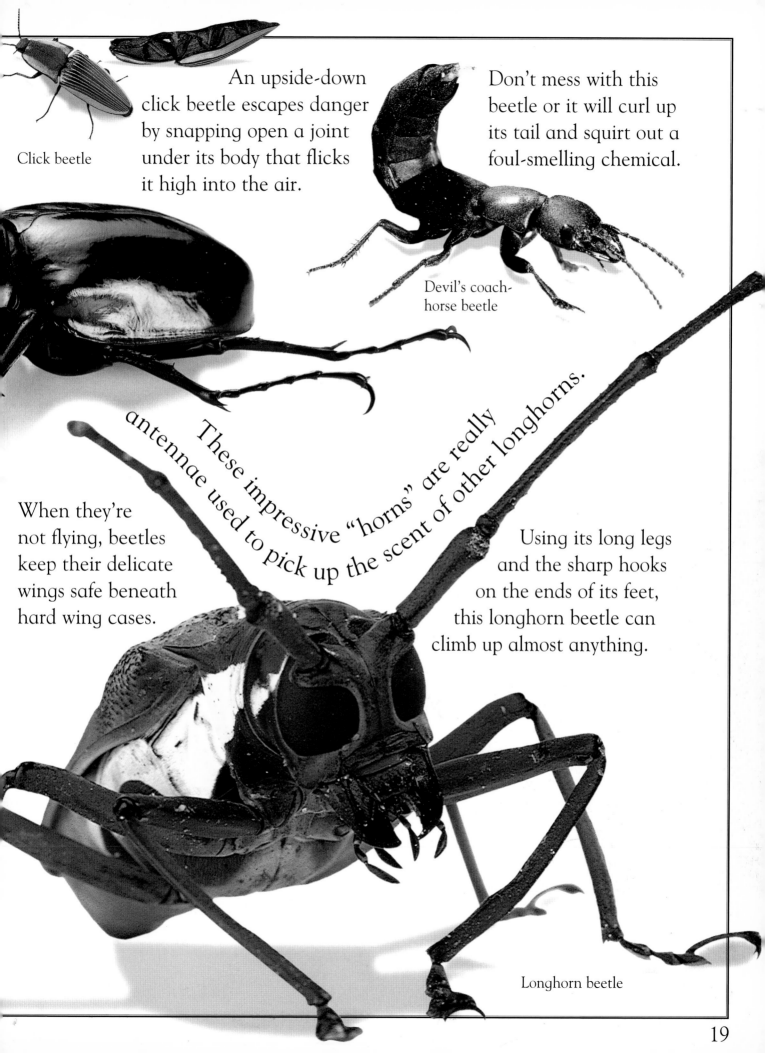

Click beetle

An upside-down click beetle escapes danger by snapping open a joint under its body that flicks it high into the air.

Don't mess with this beetle or it will curl up its tail and squirt out a foul-smelling chemical.

Devil's coach-horse beetle

These impressive "horns" are really antennae used to pick up the scent of other longhorns.

When they're not flying, beetles keep their delicate wings safe beneath hard wing cases.

Using its long legs and the sharp hooks on the ends of its feet, this longhorn beetle can climb up almost anything.

Longhorn beetle

19

BEASTLY BUGS

All bugs have tube-shaped mouths designed for sucking liquids. Some live entirely on the sugary sap in plants, while others suck the fluids out of other insects or larger animals.

Some scientists think that this bug's strange-shaped head and big eyes help it to scare away predators.

Shield bug

Shield bug

Shield bug

Bright colours warn predators that a bug tastes bad, while green helps it to hide.

When a lantern bug is disturbed, it lets off a nasty smell, flashes its bright wings, and shakes its rattly head.